The Official
FIFA WORLD CUP
Qatar2022™

Kids' Fact File

© FIFA TM

All set for kick-off!

Qatar is preparing to host the planet's biggest football extravaganza – the FIFA World Cup Qatar 2022. The 64-game competition kicks off on 21 November, with the curtain coming down on the tournament on 18 December. To help you limber up for this global football festival, we bring you the *FIFA World Cup 2022 Kids' Fact File*, which is packed full of everything you need to know about the tournament.

CONTENTS

◄ Defending champions France are considered among the favourites to triumph at Qatar 2022.

5

Welcome to the FIFA World Cup 2022

Qatar 2022 promises a plentiful supply of superstar talents, amazing goals, memorable matches and much more besides. The action is set to get under way in Group A on 21 November, as the world's leading national teams begin their quest to capture the most prestigious prize in global football. France are bidding to retain the crown they claimed at the 2018 FIFA World Cup Russia. A host of other contenders, including Brazil, Argentina, Belgium, Germany, Spain and England, will also be vying for tournament glory.

After being awarded the FIFA World Cup 2022 hosting duties in 2010, Qatar has worked hard to make it a tournament to remember. The beautiful Gulf nation has built breathtaking new stadiums in five cities – the supporters in the stands and the millions watching back home will be treated to a spectacle, with legends including Lionel Messi, Harry Kane, Kylian Mbappé, Neymar and Kevin De Bruyne set to light up the 22nd edition of the FIFA World Cup.

Football fever

Every time the FIFA World Cup rolls around, the passion for the tournament reaches fever pitch. The first edition was held in Uruguay in 1930 and the hosts made home advantage count, overcoming Argentina in the final. Since then, only seven other countries have tasted FIFA World Cup glory. Which team do you think will lift the trophy this time round?

▶ Argentina's Lionel Messi is set to appear in his fifth FIFA World Cup at Qatar 2022.

Every FIFA World Cup final

2018	France 4-2 Croatia
2014	Germany 1-0 Argentina (AET)
2010	Spain 1-0 Netherlands (AET)
2006	Italy 1-1 France*
2002	Brazil 2-0 Germany
1998	France 3-0 Brazil
1994	Brazil 0-0 Italy**
1990	West Germany 1-0 Argentina
1986	Argentina 3-2 West Germany
1982	Italy 3-1 West Germany
1978	Argentina 3-1 Netherlands (AET)
1974	West Germany 2-1 Netherlands
1970	Brazil 4-1 Italy
1966	England 4-2 West Germany (AET)
1962	Brazil 3-1 Czechoslovakia
1958	Brazil 5-2 Sweden
1954	West Germany 3-2 Hungary
1950	Uruguay 2-1 Brazil***
1938	Italy 4-2 Hungary
1934	Italy 2-1 Czechoslovakia (AET)
1930	Uruguay 4-2 Argentina

* Italy won 5-3 on penalties.
** Brazil won 3-2 on penalties.
*** The winners were determined in the final round of games of the second group stage.
    AET = after extra time

Qatar 2022 tournament format

On 21 November, the eyes of the world will be on Al Thumama Stadium, where Senegal and the Netherlands will contest the first game of the tournament. As hosts, Qatar qualified automatically for the finals and will feature in the day's second match against Ecuador. The other 31 countries booked their place after getting through a regional qualifying campaign, which for some teams started way back in June 2019.

Group games

The 32 teams have been drawn into eight groups of four. These are lettered from A to H. Four group games will be played on each day up until 2 December. Each team will meet all three opponents in their group. Following these matches, the teams that take the top two spots in their respective group will progress to the knockout stage.

It's a knockout!

The teams that reach the round of 16 face the pressure of knockout games. In this stage, group winners take on the runners-up from another group (see the match schedule on pages 62-63). If the scores are tied after normal time, the teams play 30 minutes of extra time. If that fails to break the deadlock, a penalty shoot-out will decide who goes through. The winners advance to the quarter-finals as they bid to reach the semi-finals and ultimately book their spot in the final, to be played on 18 December. The two beaten semi-finalists will contest the third-place play-off on 17 December.

▼ Germany celebrate winning their fourth World Cup title after beating Argentina 1-0 at Brazil 2014.

The ultimate prize

The national teams will battle it out across 64 games in a bid to get their hands on the FIFA World Cup Trophy. This iconic prize stands 36.8cm tall and weighs a little over 6kg. On 18 December, the winning captain will have the honour of lifting it first, sparking joyous celebrations with his team and fans!

Original trophy

The Jules Rimet Trophy was awarded to the countries that won the editions played between 1930 and 1970. When Brazil claimed the title for a third time in 1970, they were allowed to keep the trophy permanently. Sadly, it was stolen in 1983 and never seen again.

Stunning stadiums

Reflecting the unique location of the FIFA World Cup 2022 – the first edition to be staged in the Middle East – the venues in Qatar draw on their surroundings and links to a rich history and culture. Qatari attractions range from Doha's stunning skyscrapers and waterfront restaurants to the deserts around Al Rayyan and the country's beaches, ancient forts, towers and rock-carving sites.

© FIFA TM

Ahmad Bin Ali Stadium

City: Al Rayyan ◆ **Capacity:** 40,000

Looks like: an ultra-modern arena that respects its environment.

Design inspiration: the surrounding sand dunes found across the deserts of Al Rayyan.

Did you know? The stadium was officially opened exactly two years before the FIFA World Cup 2022 final, which is to be played on 18 December. Once the tournament is over, the local football team, Al-Rayyan Sports Club, will take up residence in the stadium.

Al Thumama Stadium

City: Doha ◆ **Capacity:** 40,000

Looks like: a traditional Arab headwear piece known as a *gahfiya*.

Design inspiration: the popular cap worn by men throughout the Middle East.

Did you know? Although the design is based on the *gahfiya*, Al Thumama Stadium is actually named after a native Qatari tree that grows in the area. There are also plans to develop a hotel and sports clinic at the stadium after the finals.

▼ The Lusail Stadium rises like a giant golden bowl and is surrounded by a moat.

Lusail Stadium

City: Lusail ◆ **Capacity:** 80,000

Looks like: the ideal venue for the FIFA World Cup 2022 final.

Design inspiration: the stadium design is based on the decorative motifs that feature on bowls across the Arab world.

Did you know? Lusail Stadium is the largest venue at Qatar 2022 and will host the final on 18 December. Despite it being a brand-new arena, most of the seats are set to be removed after the tournament and donated to other sporting projects around the world.

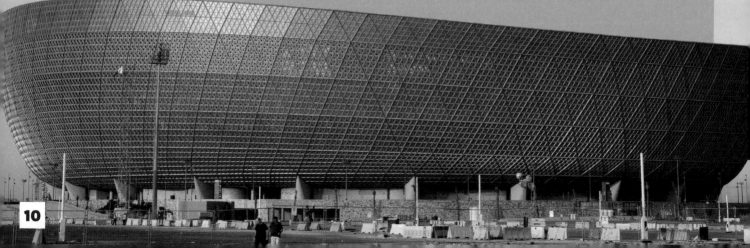

Education City Stadium (right)

City: Al Rayyan ◆ **Capacity:** 40,000

Looks like: a futuristic, innovative dome.

Design inspiration: the world-class universities that surround this arena, while consideration has also been given to green spaces.

Did you know? Opened in 2020 as one of the first of Qatar's new venues for the finals, the Education City Stadium will host the opening quarter-final match, as well as a round-of-16 match and six group games.

Al Janoub Stadium

City: Al Wakrah ◆ **Capacity:** 40,000

Looks like: a huge, stunning, shining pearl.

Design inspiration: the history of Al Wakrah, which was formerly a famous pearling village.

Did you know? Al Janoub Stadium was revealed to the world in spectacular fashion as it hosted the 2019 Amir Cup final. Al-Duhail Sports Club prevailed on a night when fireworks lit up the sky around the new arena.

Khalifa International Stadium (below)

City: Doha ◆ **Capacity:** 45,416

Looks like: Qatar's oldest football venue.

Design inspiration: revamped from its original 1970s design, its dual arches continue to sweep the skyline.

Did you know? The Khalifa International Stadium has staged high-profile matches in the past, including fixtures in the FIFA Club World Cup, Asian Games, AFC Asian Cup, Gulf Cup and Amir Cup.

Al Bayt Stadium (above)

City: Al Khor ◆ **Capacity:** 60,000

Looks like: a giant tent.

Design inspiration: a type of tent called *bayt al sha'ar* that has been historically used by nomadic people throughout Qatar and the Gulf region.

Did you know? Al Bayt Stadium will stage Qatar's opening match of the FIFA World Cup 2022. FIFA representatives have described the stadium as a unique and distinctive arena.

Stadium 974

City: Doha ◆ **Capacity:** 40,000

Looks like: shipping containers and modular building blocks.

Design inspiration: to be a highly renewable space, with the shipping containers, seats and blocks set to be removed for use elsewhere in the world.

Did you know? Stadium 974 is the first temporary venue in the tournament's history and will stage six games at the FIFA World Cup before being taken down. There are plans for the site to become a shiny waterfront development to be used by the local community.

FIFA World Cup highlights

Before we give you the lowdown on the teams competing at Qatar 2022, as well as some of the top talents poised to strut their stuff in the competition, let's take a quick look back at some crowning moments from previous FIFA World Cups.

1970
Super Canaries

The Brazil team that lined up at the 1970 FIFA World Cup were among the best sides to have ever graced the competition. Boasting stars like Pelé, Jairzinho, Roberto Rivellino and Tostão, they powered through their group and went on to reach the final, where they outclassed Italy in a 4-1 win. Captain Carlos Alberto rounded off the scoring with a thumping strike after a flowing team move.

Awards galore

A range of individual awards are up for grabs at the tournament. The top scorer receives the adidas Golden Boot, while the competition's standout player picks up the adidas Golden Ball and the outstanding goalkeeper collects the adidas Golden Glove.

1974
Top turn

Dutch hero Johan Cruyff led his country to the 1974 final with his skills, assists and goals. In a group game against Sweden, he brought a lofted, cross-field pass under control outside the opposition's penalty area, before pushing the ball behind his own standing leg to leave the defender bamboozled and allow him to send in a cross. This piece of skill became known as the Cruyff turn.

2006
Terrific teamwork

Argentina crafted an amazing team goal in a group-stage match against Serbia and Montenegro at the 2006 FIFA World Cup Germany. The move involved a series of 24 passes, lasted 56 seconds, featured no fewer than nine players and culminated in midfielder Esteban Cambiasso clipping the ball home from inside the box in what was the second goal of a 6-0 rout.

2014
Klose call

The competition marked a crowning moment in the career of Germany hitman Miroslav Klose. Not only did Germany win the trophy, but Klose scored twice to take his overall tally at FIFA World Cups to a record-breaking 16 goals, having also netted in the 2002, 2006 and 2010 editions.

2018
Six-goal thriller

Not since 1966 had a FIFA World Cup final served up six goals. France ultimately ran out 4-2 winners over Croatia in the 2018 FIFA World Cup Russia final, but it was not all plain sailing for Didier Deschamps's men. They went ahead courtesy of an own goal, but Croatia then drew level. However, the French established a 4-1 lead by the 65th minute thanks to strikes from Antoine Griezmann, Paul Pogba and teenage sensation Kylian Mbappé. A mistake by Hugo Lloris gave Croatia renewed hope, but no further goals were forthcoming as *Les Bleus* lifted the trophy.

Classy Qatar

Qatar is set for a spectacular celebration of football. The fans are ready for the big kick-off in Group A on 21 November, when the Al Bayt Stadium in Al Khor will be packed with excited supporters awaiting Qatar's first FIFA World Cup appearance.

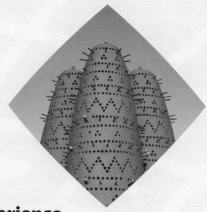

Measuring around 80km wide and 160km long, Qatar is easily the smallest nation ever to stage the world's biggest football event. Nevertheless, Qatar promises to host a grand tournament and charm visitors with its rich cultural traditions and hospitality.

Special city

Qatar is a vibrant, modern place. The capital, Doha, mixes wonderful waterside scenes with hi-tech buildings, pleasant walks and world-class shopping. Outside of Doha, the country's heritage as an ancient land of fishing and pearling shines through.

▼ The passionate Qatari fans are ready to get behind their team and help the side go far in the competition.

Souq experience

Souqs are traditional markets, where traders offer a range of regional goods to locals and visitors. They are also the site of musical and artistic performances, plus exhibitions. The Souq Waqif in Doha has been around for more than a century. Visitors can take a trip through its winding alleys, search for local handicrafts, tour the pearl stalls and stop for refreshments at a friendly café. Meanwhile, the Gold Souq and Falcon Souq offer a splash of Persian life.

Corniche cruise

The famous palm-fringed Corniche promenade is a must-see for every visitor to the country. More than 7km long, the waterside haven boasts a brilliant blend of restaurants, parks, shops, cycle paths, picnic spots, city views, cultural features and much more.

Group A
QATAR

"In 2022, we'll play the FIFA World Cup in our home country, which means we won't be intimidated." These are the words of star striker Almoez Ali in a clear statement of intent. As tournament hosts, the Qataris did not play any qualifiers, but have contested some competitive friendly games in their preparations, including a match against Portugal. Coach Félix Sánchez Bas favours a 4-3-3 set-up, but his team can adopt a more defensive 5-3-2 formation if needed. The home fans will be delighted if their team manage to pick up any points early on in Group A.

TEAM GUIDE

Captain: Hassan al Haydos
Coach: Félix Sánchez Bas
Route to Qatar: qualified automatically as hosts
Previous appearances: n/a
Best finish: n/a

Players to watch
Almoez Ali: penalty-box predator
Saad al Sheeb: fine shot-stopper
Hassan al Haydos: goalscoring no. 10

▲ Al Haydos was coached by Spain's World Cup winner Xavi Hernández at Al Sadd.

70
Ali and Al Haydos have plundered more than 70 international goals between them.

Almoez Ali has been on target at the AFC Asian Cup, the CONMEBOL *Copa América* and the Concacaf Gold Cup.

Group A

ECUADOR

An impressive 4-2 win against Uruguay in their second match in CONMEBOL qualifying helped Ecuador reach their fourth FIFA World Cup finals. Gustavo Alfaro's team kept six clean sheets in the qualifiers as their tactic of being resolute at the back and then launching quick attacks paid off. They have a mix of energetic young talent, such as winger Gonzalo Plata and defender Piero Hincapié, and experience in the shape of forward Enner Valencia and midfielder Carlos Gruezo.

📋 TEAM GUIDE

Captain: Enner Valencia
Coach: Gustavo Alfaro
Route to Qatar: fourth, CONMEBOL
Previous appearances: 3
Best finish: round of 16 (2006)

Players to watch

Enner Valencia: classy goalscorer
Gonzalo Plata: pacy and skilful
Piero Hincapié: tenacious defender

▲ Piero Hincapié has impressed in the German *Bundesliga* with Bayer Leverkusen.

6
Ecuador beat Colombia 6-1 in qualifying with six different scorers.

Enner Valencia is Ecuador's record scorer with 35 goals in 70 appearances for his country.

Group A
🏳 SENEGAL

Senegal reached their third FIFA World Cup finals following a thrilling play-off battle with Egypt in March 2022. The second leg went to penalties and the crucial spot kick was scored by their talismanic forward Sadio Mané, who had also netted the winning penalty in another shoot-out success over Egypt in the 2021 Africa Cup of Nations final. With stars from many of the world's top leagues, including Kalidou Koulibaly, Édouard Mendy and Ismaïla Sarr, the *Lions of Teranga* have plenty of skill and spirit that could take them past the group stage.

TEAM GUIDE

Captain: Kalidou Koulibaly
Coach: Aliou Cissé
Route to Qatar: winners, CAF round three
Previous appearances: 2
Best finish: quarter-finals (2002)

Players to watch
Édouard Mendy: commanding shot-stopper
Sadio Mané: lightning-quick attacker
Kalidou Koulibaly: strong central defender

▲ Édouard Mendy regularly makes big saves for Senegal.

7
Senegal scored in seven of their eight qualifying games.

Fearsome forward Sadio Mané scored at Russia 2018.

Group A
THE NETHERLANDS

Leading the Netherlands into a FIFA World Cup for the second time in his career, the experienced Louis van Gaal has plenty of stars to choose from, such as Virgil van Dijk and Georginio Wijnaldum, while Davy Klaassen was in top form in qualifying, chipping in with four goals and assists apiece. The Netherlands are likely to set up in a 4-3-3 system, with Wijnaldum, Steven Bergwijn and Klaassen almost certain to be tasked with supporting Memphis Depay in attack. Van Gaal's side will be itching to show what they are capable of on the world stage.

TEAM GUIDE

Captain: Virgil van Dijk
Coach: Louis van Gaal
Route to Qatar: winners, UEFA Group G
Previous appearances: 10
Best finish: runners-up (2010, 1978, 1974)

Players to watch

Virgil van Dijk: imposing centre-back
Georginio Wijnaldum: goalscoring midfielder
Memphis Depay: prolific in front of goal

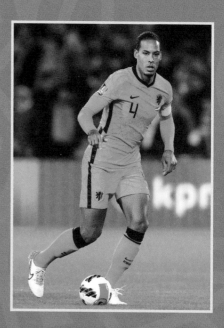

▲ Van Dijk has captained the Netherlands since 2018.

3
The Netherlands finished third at the 2014 FIFA World Cup, their last appearance at the finals.

Georginio Wijnaldum netted 26 goals in his first 85 international appearances.

Group B
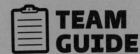 **ENGLAND**

Having reached the semi-finals of the 2018 FIFA World Cup Russia and contested the UEFA EURO 2020 final, the *Three Lions* head to Qatar brimming with confidence. Coach Gareth Southgate prefers a 4-2-3-1 system, with Harry Kane spearheading the attack and the likes of Raheem Sterling, Jack Grealish and Mason Mount in support. Declan Rice has become a key player in the holding midfield role and with talented youngsters such as Jude Bellingham and Jadon Sancho in their ranks, England are sure to keep fans on the edge of their seats.

TEAM GUIDE

Captain: Harry Kane
Coach: Gareth Southgate
Route to Qatar: winners, UEFA Group I
Previous appearances: 15
Best finish: winners (1966)

Players to watch

Harry Kane: lethal finisher
Jack Grealish: exciting playmaker
Harry Maguire: defensive leader

▲ Grealish scored his first England goal in the 5-0 FIFA World Cup qualifying win away to Andorra in October 2021.

0
England did not lose any games in qualifying for Qatar. Their last defeat in a FIFA World Cup qualifier was in 2009.

Harry Kane first wore the captain's armband for the national side in June 2017.

Group B
IR IRAN

Striker Mehdi Taremi's goal in a 1-0 qualifying win over Iraq booked IR Iran's place in Qatar and continued coach Dragan Skočić's impressive run of results. It was his 13th win from 14 games after taking charge in February 2020. IR Iran will be contesting their sixth FIFA World Cup finals and their dream now is to make the round of 16 for the first time. To do so, they need Taremi and Sardar Azmoun, who bagged 40 goals in his first 62 internationals, to continue finding the net.

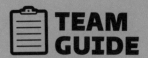

TEAM GUIDE

Captain: Ehsan Hajsafi
Coach: Dragan Skočić
Route to Qatar: winners, AFC round three Group A
Previous appearances: 5
Best finish: group stage (2018, 2014, 2006, 1998, 1978)

Players to watch

Mehdi Taremi: lively around the box
Sardar Azmoun: reliable scorer who sets up goals too
Alireza Jahanbakhsh: exciting winger

3

IR Iran are playing in their third FIFA World Cup finals in a row.

▲ Goal machine Azmoun moved to German club Bayer Leverkusen in 2022.

Mehdi Taremi was nominated for the FIFA Puskás Award in 2021 for a sublime goal he struck for Porto.

Group B
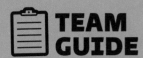 USA

After failing to qualify for Russia 2018, the USA were determined not to be left out of the action in Qatar. Europe-based stars such as attacker Christian Pulisic, defensive midfielder Tyler Adams and the versatile Giovanni Reyna have big-game experience that will be important when the group games begin. Gregg Berhalter uses an effective 4-3-3 formation, which will see youngsters such as Brenden Aaronson and Ricardo Pepi compete for a striking spot. Sergiño Dest's ability to burst forward from full-back could create chances for the team.

2026
The FIFA World Cup 2026 will be hosted by the USA, Canada and Mexico.

TEAM GUIDE

Captain: Christian Pulisic
Coach: Gregg Berhalter
Route to Qatar: third, Concacaf round three
Previous appearances: 10
Best finish: third place (1930)

Players to watch

Christian Pulisic: creative forward
Weston McKennie: midfield dynamo
Tyler Adams: midfielder with great defensive instincts

▲ Tyler Adams captained Team USA in qualifying at the age of just 22.

Christian Pulisic pulls the strings as a creative no. 10 behind the strikers.

Group C

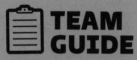

ARGENTINA

Besides their global hero Lionel Messi, *La Albiceleste* are blessed with other goalscoring talents who could play their part at Qatar 2022. Frontman Lautaro Martínez has stepped up and filled the void left by Gonzalo Higuaín, ably flanked by Messi and Ángel Di María in a 4-3-3 formation, while Giovani Lo Celso has established himself as a key playmaker. Coach Lionel Scaloni has drafted in several new players alongside the team's mainstays. After lifting the CONMEBOL *Copa América* 2021, spirits are high in the Argentina camp.

TEAM GUIDE

Captain: Lionel Messi
Coach: Lionel Scaloni
Route to Qatar: runners-up, CONMEBOL
Previous appearances: 17
Best finish: winners (1986, 1978)

Players to watch

Lionel Messi: goals and creativity aplenty
Lautaro Martínez: proven scorer
Cristian Romero: key centre-back who times tackles brilliantly

▲ Recent additions like Romero have turned in some impressive displays.

9

Argentina's first 20 goals in qualifying were scored by nine different players.

Striker Lautaro Martínez struck seven goals in 17 qualifiers for Qatar 2022.

Group C

SAUDI ARABIA

The *Green Falcons* proudly reached Qatar 2022 with two games to spare in AFC round three Group B. Coached by the experienced Frenchman Hervé Renard, who has won the Africa Cup of Nations with Côte d'Ivoire and Zambia, Saudi Arabia are a well-drilled team and regularly line up in a 4-2-3-1 formation. Saleh al Shehri is usually the striker picked to lead the attack, supported by the creative skills of Salem al Dawsari, Sami al Najei and Fahad al Muwallad. The defensive midfield work of captain Salman al Faraj cannot be underestimated either.

TEAM GUIDE

Captain: Salman al Faraj
Coach: Hervé Renard
Route to Qatar: winners, AFC round three Group B
Previous appearances: 5
Best finish: round of 16 (1994)

Players to watch

Salman al-Faraj: midfield schemer
Firas al Buraikan: talented young forward
Saleh al Shehri: fearsome striker

▲ Captain Salman al Faraj scored at the 2018 FIFA World Cup.

2018

Coach Hervé Renard was in charge of Morocco at the 2018 FIFA World Cup.

Qatar 2022 presents a wonderful opportunity for 22-year-old forward Firas al Buraikan to shine.

23

 MEXICO

Can Mexico finally go beyond the round of 16 again, having fallen at that stage at the last seven editions? The goals of Raúl Jiménez and attacking creativity of Hirving Lozano and Héctor Herrera will be crucial in their quest. Mexico kept eight clean sheets in 14 qualifying games and more top-class defensive displays from veteran goalkeeper Guillermo Ochoa and defenders including Johan Vásquez, César Montes and Héctor Moreno are needed to shut out the opposition strikers in Qatar. Backed by passionate fans, Mexico will give everything in their group.

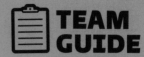 **TEAM GUIDE**

Captain: Andrés Guardado
Coach: Gerardo Martino
Route to Qatar: runners-up, Concacaf round three
Previous appearances: 16
Best finish: quarter-finals (1986, 1970)

Players to watch

Raúl Jiménez: penalty-box predator
Hirving Lozano: versatile winger or forward
Edson Álvarez: midfielder who shields the defence

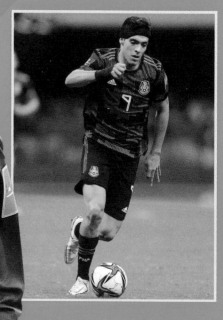

▲ Raúl Jiménez is looking for his first FIFA World Cup finals goals at his third tournament.

8
This is Mexico's eighth FIFA World Cup in a row, a run going back to 1994.

Reliable midfielder Edson Álvarez helped Mexico win the Concacaf Gold Cup in 2019.

Group C
POLAND

Fans want to see the world's best players at a FIFA World Cup. This is why they will welcome Poland, led by the incredible Robert Lewandowski, in Qatar. The attacking ace scored in the 2-0 play-off victory against Sweden and is now ready to bag his first finals goal after failing to do so four years ago. Coach Czesław Michniewicz, who took charge in January 2022, will draw on the experience of players such as Wojciech Szczęsny and Grzegorz Krychowiak, while fresher faces, including Matty Cash and Karol Świderski, will add plenty of energy to his squad.

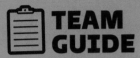

TEAM GUIDE

Captain: Robert Lewandowski
Coach: Czesław Michniewicz
Route to Qatar: runners-up, UEFA Group I; play-offs
Previous appearances: 8
Best finish: third place (1982, 1974)

Players to watch

Robert Lewandowski: world-class striker
Arkadiusz Milik: pacy forward with a sweet left foot
Jan Bednarek: calm in central defence

75

Robert Lewandowski's goal against Sweden in the play-off final was his 75th for Poland.

▲ Lewandowski has scored more than 500 career goals at club level.

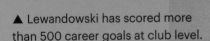

Arkadiusz Milik's playing style has been compared to that of his compatriot Lewandowski.

Group D
🇫🇷 FRANCE

France have enjoyed phenomenal success over the past six years under coach Didier Deschamps. *Les Bleus* captured the FIFA World Cup Trophy in 2018, the UEFA Nations League crown in 2021 and finished runners-up at UEFA EURO 2016. The squad is blessed in every department. Goalkeeper Hugo Lloris commands his penalty area with impressive authority, centre-back Raphaël Varane snuffs out any danger and goals can fly in from the likes of Antoine Griezmann, Kylian Mbappé and Karim Benzema. Can Deschamps lead *Les Bleus* to another world crown?

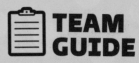

TEAM GUIDE

Captain: Hugo Lloris
Coach: Didier Deschamps
Route to Qatar: winners, UEFA Group D
Previous appearances: 15
Best finish: winners (2018, 1998)

Players to watch

Kylian Mbappé: energetic, pacy forward
N'Golo Kanté: midfield lynchpin
Raphaël Varane: assured presence at the back

▲Varane played every minute in France's victorious 2018 FIFA World Cup campaign.

2017
The year Mbappé made his senior international debut at the tender age of 18.

Kylian Mbappé netted in the 2018 FIFA World Cup final and struck the winner in the UEFA Nations League showpiece against Spain in 2021.

Group D
DENMARK

Kasper Hjulmand's men emerged the dark horses at UEFA EURO 2020, where they were narrowly edged out by England in the semi-finals, and their performance levels have remained high as they come into this tournament. The Danes are driven by the midfield talents of Thomas Delaney and Pierre-Emile Højbjerg, with a sprinkle of goalscoring magic coming from the boots of Kasper Dolberg and Yussuf Poulsen. Denmark boast the ability to alter their set-up depending on their opposition – a tactical nous that is sure to serve them well in Qatar.

TEAM GUIDE

Captain: Simon Kjær
Coach: Kasper Hjulmand
Route to Qatar: winners, UEFA Group F
Previous appearances: 5
Best finish: quarter-finals (1998)

Players to watch

Simon Kjær: powerful centre-back
Pierre-Emile Højbjerg: all-action midfielder
Kasper Dolberg: silky-skilled forward

▲ Dolberg scored twice in the qualifier against Moldova in March 2021.

8
Denmark kept eight successive clean sheets during their Qatar 2022 qualifying campaign.

Simon Kjær has played his club football in Denmark, Italy, Germany, France, Turkey and Spain.

Group D
 TUNISIA

At Russia 2018, Tunisia's first group game was a heart-breaking injury-time defeat to England. Four years on, they are determined to make a bright start as they chase a coveted place in the round of 16. Wahbi Khazri will play an important role once again and his guile and attacking vision, coupled with the goals of Naïm Sliti and Youssef Msakni, give the *Eagles of Carthage* enough firepower to trouble any opposition. If their defence remains as strong as it was in early 2022, then new coach Jalel Kadri will be hopeful of a top- two finish in the group.

6

Tunisia's tough defence kept six clean sheets on the road to Qatar 2022.

📋 TEAM GUIDE

Captain: Youssef Msakni
Coach: Jalel Kadri
Route to Qatar: winners, CAF round three
Previous appearances: 5
Best finish: group stage (2018, 2006, 2002, 1998, 1978)

Players to watch
Youssef Msakni: tricky wing play
Wahbi Khazri: intelligent forward
Ali Maâloul: classy left-back

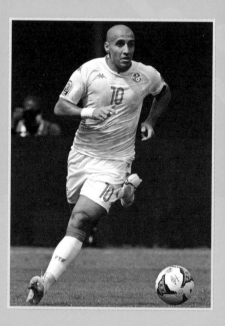

▲ Popular attacking midfielder/ forward Wahbi Khazri netted three goals to help Tunisia reach the finals.

Watch out for skilful no. 7 Youssef Msakni driving the *Eagles of Carthage* forward.

Group E
🇪🇸 SPAIN

There is no doubt that *La Roja* boast a squad that is good enough to secure glory once again, following the country's heroics at the 2010 FIFA World Cup South Africa. Coach Luis Enrique has shown a real willingness to select exciting youngsters, such as midfielders Pedri and Gavi, and combine their enthusiasm with experienced heads like Sergio Busquets, as well as Koke, Jordi Alba and Álvaro Morata. Spain are known for their neat, possession-based style and if they can rediscover a cutting edge, the route to tournament glory could really open up for them.

12

Qatar 2022 will see Spain feature at their 12th FIFA World Cup in a row.

📋 TEAM GUIDE

Captain: Sergio Busquets
Coach: Luis Enrique
Route to Qatar: winners, UEFA Group B
Previous appearances: 15
Best finish: winners (2010)

Players to watch
Ferran Torres: eye-catching attacking starlet
Pedri: talented young midfielder
Aymeric Laporte: defensive rock

▲ Pedri will be using his slick attacking skills to unlock opposition defences in Qatar.

Barcelona's young forward Ferran Torres notched four goals in six qualifying matches.

Group E
GERMANY

Germany's shock display at the last FIFA World Cup is firmly behind them. Hansi Flick took charge after UEFA EURO 2020 and the team now look like the Germany of old – free-scoring, disciplined and creative. Youngsters Jamal Musiala and Karim Adeyemi have been great additions to their attack since 2021, but it was the likes of Manuel Neuer, Mats Hummels and Leon Goretzka who helped to steer the Germans to the finals. Timo Werner, Serge Gnabry, Kai Havertz and Thomas Müller could really bag lots of goals if Germany hit the ground running in Qatar.

TEAM GUIDE

Captain: Manuel Neuer
Coach: Hansi Flick
Route to Qatar: winners, UEFA Group J
Previous appearances: 19
Best finish: winners (2014, 1990, 1974, 1954)

Players to watch

Serge Gnabry: dangerous attacking presence
Kai Havertz: capable of incisive forward runs
Timo Werner: hard-working frontman

▲ Star striker Werner lifted the 2021 UEFA Champions League crown with London side Chelsea.

1
Germany were the first team to qualify for Qatar 2022.

Serge Gnabry claimed five goals and two assists in eight qualifiers.

Group E
🇯🇵 JAPAN

A 2-0 win over Australia in March 2022 confirmed Japan's place at Qatar 2022. It was a tricky campaign for the *Samurai Blue*, who suffered early defeats to Oman and Saudi Arabia before bouncing back to claim a spot at their seventh FIFA World Cup in a row. Liverpool's Takumi Minamino and Genk's Junya Ito can conjure goals and assists, supported by the experienced Yuya Osako. Meanwhile, Kaoru Mitoma made a name for himself in qualifying with both goals against Australia and could be a danger from the bench.

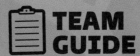

TEAM GUIDE

Captain: Maya Yoshida
Coach: Hajime Moriyasu
Route to Qatar: runners-up, AFC round three Group B
Previous appearances: 6
Best finish: round of 16 (2018, 2010, 2002)

Players to watch

Takumi Minamino: confident around the box
Maya Yoshida: marshals the backline
Takehiro Tomiyasu: versatile defender

58
The number of goals Japan scored in qualifying for Qatar 2022.

▲ Arsenal's Takehiro Tomiyasu made his Japan debut at just 19 years old.

Qatar 2022 will be Takumi Minamino's first FIFA World Cup.

Group F
🇧🇪 BELGIUM

Does this year's tournament represent Belgium's best chance of finally lifting the FIFA World Cup Trophy? Their third-place finish at Russia 2018 was impressive, but with Eden Hazard, Kevin De Bruyne and Romelu Lukaku arguably approaching the twilight of their careers, many fans believe it is a case of now or never for the *Red Devils*. Coach Roberto Martínez has been at the helm for six years and his tactical nous and the players' natural ability combine to make the Belgians a force to be reckoned with.

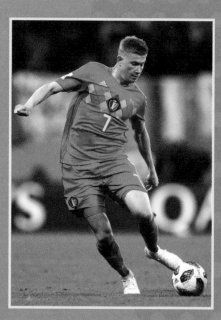

▲ Kevin De Bruyne is part of Belgium's so-called "golden generation", which also includes captain Eden Hazard.

1
Belgium first topped the FIFA/Coca-Cola World Ranking in 2015.

Romelu Lukaku netted at both the 2018 and 2014 FIFA World Cups.

Group F

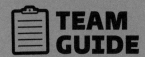 # CANADA

Spearheaded by coach John Herdman, who has previously managed Canada and New Zealand at the FIFA Women's World Cup, the *Canucks* are looking forward to being back on the biggest stage after 36 years. Their squad is full of top players, including versatile left-sided star Alphonso Davies and clinical striker Cyle Larin. Jonathan David, Lucas Cavallini and Junior Hoilett add more firepower going forward and with hugely experienced captain Atiba Hutchinson offering a cool head in midfield, Canada will set their sights on reaching the knockout stage in Qatar.

1986
The year Canada last played at the FIFA World Cup.

TEAM GUIDE

Captain: Atiba Hutchinson
Coach: John Herdman
Route to Qatar: winners, Concacaf round three
Previous appearances: 1
Best finish: group stage (1986)

Players to watch

Alphonso Davies: skilful left-footed ace
Cyle Larin: dangerous in the penalty box
Junior Hoilett: hard-working winger

▲ Cyle Larin is Canada's top striker, having bagged 24 goals in his first 50 appearances.

Alphonso Davies stars for Bayern Munich in Germany's *Bundesliga*.

Group F

MOROCCO

Morocco cruised through qualifying and were the only team to win every game in CAF round two. In round three, their 5-2 aggregate triumph over Congo DR ensured the *Atlas Lions* made it back-to-back appearances at the FIFA World Cup. Coach Vahid Halilhodžić is happy to vary his formation depending on the opposition, using a defensive 5-3-2 to keep it tight or switching to a 4-3-1-2 to attack. Morocco have not reached the knockout phase since 1986, but their team spirit and solid organisation give them a chance of doing that in Qatar.

TEAM GUIDE

Captain: Romain Saïss
Coach: Vahid Halilhodžić
Route to Qatar: winners, CAF round three
Previous appearances: 5
Best finish: round of 16 (1986)

Players to watch

Achraf Hakimi: versatile right-back
Youssef En-Nesyri: a threat in the penalty box
Yassine Bounou: highly talented goalkeeper

▲ Yassine Bounou conceded just one goal in the CAF round two qualifiers.

25
The number of goals Morocco scored in the eight games they played to book their finals spot.

Achraf Hakimi has won honours with Paris Saint-Germain, Inter Milan, Borussia Dortmund and Real Madrid.

Group F

CROATIA

A late own goal secured the 1-0 win over Russia that helped Croatia seal qualification for Qatar 2022. The runners-up last time round have retained the nucleus of the side that featured in the showpiece against France, with Dejan Lovren continuing to marshal the defence, the legendary Luka Modrić bringing the midfield magic and wideman Ivan Perišić giving the opposition rearguard plenty to think about. Captain Modrić has been the chief creative force for the past 16 years and at 37, he continues to set the team's tempo.

TEAM GUIDE

Captain: Luka Modrić
Coach: Zlatko Dalić
Route to Qatar: winners, UEFA Group H
Previous appearances: 5
Best finish: runners-up (2018)

Players to watch

Luka Modrić: midfield master
Ivan Perišić: lethal left foot
Marcelo Brozović: patrols the midfield

▲ Modrić scored three times during the qualifiers for Qatar 2022.

4
Luka Modrić is preparing for his fourth FIFA World Cup.

Often deployed as a winger, Ivan Perišić has 32 international strikes to his name.

35

Group G

 **BRAZIL**

The five-time champions look strong in every area as they bid to secure their first FIFA World Cup triumph in 20 years. The mesmerising Neymar spearheads the attack, with Premier League pair Gabriel Jesus and Roberto Firmino adding extra sparkle around him. Casemiro anchors the midfield excellently, while Marquinhos continues to shine at the back, ahead of Alisson and Ederson, who fight it out for the goalkeeper spot. Led by coach Tite, Brazil qualified with six games to spare. The team are a well-oiled machine that can attack at breakneck speed and with devastating efficiency.

▲The versatile Jesus is capable of playing in several attacking positions.

21
Brazil are the only country to have featured at all 21 FIFA World Cups.

Superstar Neymar hit a hat-trick against Peru in Brazil's second qualifying game.

Group G

SERBIA

Serbia booked their place at Qatar 2022 thanks to a dramatic 90th-minute winner in their final qualifying game. While reliable frontman Aleksandar Mitrović was the hero that night, Serbia have other game-changers in their side, too. Captain Dušan Tadić has an eye for an assist, Sergej Milinković-Savić is a powerhouse in midfield and 22-year-old forward Dušan Vlahović has impressed since winning his first cap in 2020. Serbia failed to reach the round of 16 in their previous two tournament appearances – in 2018 and 2010 – and have made this their target in 2022.

Dušan Tadić recorded two goals and six assists in qualifying.

TEAM GUIDE

Captain: Dušan Tadić
Coach: Dragan Stojković
Route to Qatar: winners, UEFA Group A
Previous appearances: 12
Best finish: fourth place (1962, 1930 – as Yugoslavia)

Players to watch
Aleksandar Mitrović: fox in the box
Dušan Tadić: assist machine
Dušan Vlahović: exciting young forward

▲ Dušan Vlahović is set to appear at his first FIFA World Cup after impressing in Italy's *Serie A* throughout the 2021-22 season.

5
Mitrović took all of five minutes to find the net in Serbia's second group-stage game at the 2018 FIFA World Cup.

37

Group G
🇨🇭 SWITZERLAND

Switzerland were the surprise package as they won their qualifying group, edging out UEFA EURO 2020 champions Italy and going unbeaten in their eight outings. They also stunned France at the latest European Championship, before narrowly losing to Spain. While they may lack a superstar name, the skills and experience of Xherdan Shaqiri, Granit Xhaka's work ethic and the unselfish forward play of Breel Embolo mean that anyone who underestimates the Swiss at Qatar 2022 does so at their peril.

TEAM GUIDE

Captain: Granit Xhaka
Coach: Murat Yakin
Route to Qatar: winners, UEFA Group C
Previous appearances: 11
Best finish: quarter-finals (1954, 1938, 1934)

Players to watch

Xherdan Shaqiri: all-action attacker
Haris Seferović: potent penalty-area predator
Granit Xhaka: high-octane midfielder

▲ Qatar 2022 will mark Seferović's third appearance at a FIFA World Cup.

100
Influential midfielder Granit Xhaka earned his 100th cap in March 2022.

Granit Xhaka played in all ten of Switzerland's 2014 FIFA World Cup qualification campaign matches.

Group G

CAMEROON

A dramatic injury-time winner from Karl Toko Ekambi in extra time during Cameroon's play-off against Algeria ensured the nation reached their eighth FIFA World Cup. Coach Rigobert Song played in four editions of the tournament, from 1994 to 2010, and will look to inspire Cameroon to the knockout stage with his touchline passion. André Onana, Michael Ngadeu-Ngadjui, André-Frank Zambo Anguissa and Vincent Aboubakar form the spine of the team, with the onus on Toko Ekambi and Eric Maxim Choupo-Moting to chalk up goals and assists.

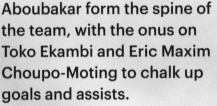

TEAM GUIDE

Captain: Vincent Aboubakar
Coach: Rigobert Song
Route to Qatar: winners, CAF round three
Previous appearances: 7
Best finish: quarter-finals (1990)

Players to watch
Vincent Aboubakar: experienced goal poacher
Karl Toko Ekambi: accomplished striker and passer
André Onana: dominant presence in goal

▲ Goalkeeper André Onana made his name playing for European giants Ajax in the *Eredivisie*.

8
Cameroon are appearing at their eighth FIFA World Cup, which is a record for an African nation.

Karl Toko Ekambi scored three goals in Cameroon's qualifying campaign for Qatar 2022.

PORTUGAL

Portugal needed a play-off win over North Macedonia to reach Qatar 2022 after Serbia took top spot in UEFA Group A. With a superstar squad featuring attacking greats such as Cristiano Ronaldo, Diogo Jota, João Félix and Bruno Fernandes, they will be a force to be reckoned with and have eyes on making at least the quarter-finals. Rúben Dias is Portugal's rock at the back and the nation has a wave of exciting players who were not around for the victorious UEFA EURO 2016 tournament. Playing against this team is always a tough test.

TEAM GUIDE

Captain: Cristiano Ronaldo
Coach: Fernando Santos
Route to Qatar: runners-up, UEFA Group A; play-offs
Previous appearances: 7
Best finish: third (1966)

Players to watch

Cristiano Ronaldo: supreme goal machine
Rúben Dias: experienced and ever-reliable centre-back
Diogo Jota: clever attacking movement

▲ Rúben Dias leads the backline and is known for the quality of his long-range passes.

3
The Manchester City trio of Bernardo Silva, João Cancelo and Rúben Dias are key players for the national team.

Cristiano Ronaldo holds the record for goals (115) in men's international football. Will he add to his astonishing tally at Qatar 2022?

Group H
 **GHANA**

The *Black Stars* are back at the FIFA World Cup finals after missing out four years ago. Captain André Ayew now has over 100 caps for Ghana and will pose a constant goal threat from his wide attacking position. His younger brother, Jordan, likes to link with him in the final third, and with Thomas Partey ready to burst forward from midfield, Ghana's counter-attacks are a key part of their tactics. Leicester City defender Daniel Amartey is expected to be the centre-back charged with organising the back four in Qatar.

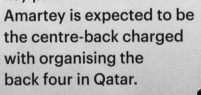 **2010**
Ghana will be keen to repeat their heroics from 12 years ago, when they reached the quarter-finals.

📋 TEAM GUIDE

Captain: André Ayew
Coach: Otto Addo
Route to Qatar: winners, CAF round three
Previous appearances: 3
Best finish: quarter-finals (2010)

Players to watch
André Ayew: inspirational captain
Thomas Partey: powerful midfielder
Jordan Ayew: cool and composed in front of goal

▲ Thomas Partey has improved his game since moving to the English Premier League in 2020.

Jordan Ayew plays as a forward for English Premier League club Crystal Palace.

41

Group H
 URUGUAY

Once Diego Alonso took charge in December 2021, a three-game winning streak secured Uruguay's place at Qatar 2022. It will be the fourth FIFA World Cup finals for stars Diego Godín, Luis Suárez and Edinson Cavani. They remain crucial to Uruguay's hopes and with Rodrigo Bentancur and Federico Valverde adding bite in midfield, *La Celeste* will once again be an entertaining team to watch. The legendary strike pairing of Suárez and Cavani will be desperate to seize their last chance of glory on the world stage.

120
Luis Suárez and Edinson Cavani have scored over 120 international goals combined.

▲ Diego Godín is an aerial presence in both penalty boxes.

Luis Suárez has netted 29 goals in FIFA World Cup qualifiers.

Group H

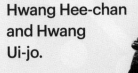

KOREA REPUBLIC

It is a perfect ten for Korea Republic as they have now reached a tenth consecutive FIFA World Cup. Coach Paulo Bento has been leading the team for more than four years and has proved to be a versatile tactician, using a 4-3-3 or 4-4-2 formation. The defence is guided by the experienced Kim Young-gwon and the midfield is powered by Lee Jae-sung. Superstar Son Heung-min leads the attack, ably supported by Hwang Hee-chan and Hwang Ui-jo.

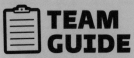

TEAM GUIDE

Captain: Son Heung-min
Coach: Paulo Bento
Route to Qatar: runners-up, AFC round three Group A
Previous appearances: 10
Best finish: semi-finals (2002)

Players to watch

Son Heung-min: world-class forward
Hwang Hee-chan: incisive through-balls
Hwang Ui-jo: impressive link-up play

▲ Hwang Hee-chan has impressed for Wolverhampton Wanderers in the English Premier League.

3
Son Heung-min has already netted three goals at the FIFA World Cup.

Hwang Ui-jo uses his pace as a centre-forward or playing in a wide role.

The final three

Twenty-nine of the 32 teams knew they would be heading to the finals when the draw for Qatar 2022 was made in Doha in April. The other three places were still up for grabs in a series of exciting play-offs that culminated in June. These games provided a final chance to join the football festival.

Tense times

Australia, Costa Rica, New Zealand, Peru, Scotland, Ukraine, the United Arab Emirates and Wales were involved in the action in June. Austria, the Czech Republic, Italy, North Macedonia, Sweden and Turkey had already failed in their play-off involvement. For four-time FIFA World Cup winners Italy, their semi-final play-off loss to North Macedonia reopened the wounds from the defeat to Sweden in the play-offs for the 2018 FIFA World Cup. These upsets show how tough it can be for even the biggest teams to earn a place at the finals.

▼ The draw for the finals was held on 1 April at the grand Doha Exhibition and Convention Center.

Group A		
QATAR		
~~UADOR~~		
~~NEGAL~~		
~~NETHE~~RLANDS		

Group B		
ENGLAND		
IR IRAN		
USA		
EUROPEAN PLAY-OFF		

Group C		
~~ARGE~~NTINA		
~~SAUDI~~ ARABIA		
~~ME~~XICO		
~~POL~~AND		

Group D		
FRANCE		
IC PLAY-OFF 1		
DENMARK		
TUNISIA		

Wales talisman Gareth Bale put on a stunning display against Austria to help his team win a place in a play-off final in June.

Memorable matches

Play-off matches have provided plenty of drama and excitement in the lead-up to previous editions of the FIFA World Cup. Most notably, double world champions Uruguay played four play-off ties in a row in their bid to advance to the tournament in 2014, 2010, 2006 and 2002. They won three, only missing out in 2006. Australia and Peru were part of the play-off games for Qatar 2022 and both won decisive matches four years ago to reach Russia 2018 at the final time of asking.

Christian Cueva twice scored winners against Venezuela on Peru's path to a place in the play-offs for Qatar 2022.

Top trio

In the boxes below, you can fill in the three countries that qualified for the FIFA World Cup 2022 after their success in the play-offs in June. Congratulations to these nations for sealing the final spots at the biggest football event on the planet!

1 ....
2 ....
3 ....

Group F
BELGIUM
CANADA
MOROCCO
CROATIA

Group G
BRAZIL
SERBIA
SWITZERLAND
CAMEROON

Group H
PORTUGAL
GHANA
URUGUAY
KOREA REPUBLIC

FIFA WORLD CUP
Qatar 2022

Final Draw

LIONEL MESSI

Country: Argentina ◆ **Club:** Paris Saint-Germain

Date of birth: 24 June 1987

 160 caps 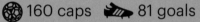 81 goals

The sight of Argentina's legendary no. 10 slaloming his way past defenders with the ball glued to his feet before slotting home another glorious goal is one we have become used to over the past two decades. At 35, this could well be Lionel Messi's final shot at glory on the world stage. He scored the opening goal in Argentina's qualifying campaign, against Ecuador, before claiming the match ball in the 3-0 win over Bolivia. He also led from the front as *La Albiceleste* secured a goalless draw against Brazil to book their place in the tournament. Now it is time to sit back and enjoy Messi's magic!

6

Messi has netted six times at FIFA World Cups.

ROMELU LUKAKU

Country: Belgium ◆ **Club:** Chelsea
Date of birth: 13 May 1993

🏐 101 caps 👟 68 goals

As incredible as it may seem, Romelu Lukaku has indeed notched 68 goals in just over a century of appearances for Belgium. However, his goalscoring exploits are perhaps not all that surprising considering he has the likes of Kevin De Bruyne, Eden Hazard and Axel Witsel on hand to provide the ammunition. And when given a chance in the box, the powerful Chelsea hitman usually finds the back of the net. Lukaku struck five times in just four qualifying games and if he can beat his four-goal haul from Russia 2018, Belgium have a good chance of progressing to the latter stages in Qatar.

KYLIAN MBAPPÉ

Country: France ◆ **Club:** Paris Saint-Germain
Date of birth: 20 December 1998

🏐 54 caps 👟 26 goals

Kylian Mbappé scored five times in six appearances to help France qualify for Qatar. But there is so much more to his game than goals. The striking sensation works incredibly hard in attacking areas, where he uses his electric pace and intricate footwork to pull defenders out of position and fashion goalscoring opportunities. Mbappé has already written his name into FIFA World Cup folklore following his performances in *Les Bleus*' run to glory in 2018. He is now a more accomplished forward and primed to make an even bigger impact. Let the show begin.

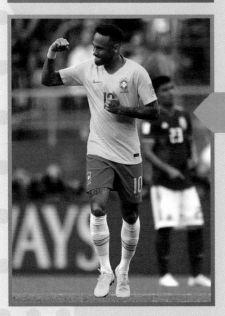

NEYMAR

Country: Brazil ◆ **Club:** Paris Saint-Germain
Date of birth: 5 February 1992

🏐 117 caps 👟 71 goals

At Qatar 2022, Neymar is set to spearhead Brazil's attack for the third time at a FIFA World Cup. He was a pivotal figure for his country on the road to the tournament, having netted in qualifiers against Paraguay, Ecuador, Peru, Uruguay and Chile, and will be itching to add to his six-goal tally on the world's biggest stage. As a leading light for one of the tournament's favourites, Neymar will be under pressure to deliver in Qatar. Fortunately, he has all the tools to handle big occasions and would even appear to thrive on the expectation levels.

FIFA World Cup player watch: FORWARDS

HARRY KANE

Country: England ◆ **Club:** Tottenham
Date of birth: 28 July 1993

 69 caps 👟 49 goals

Harry Kane heads to Qatar with a reputation as a formidable world-class forward. He finished joint-top scorer in the European qualifiers, bagging 12 goals in just eight outings as the *Three Lions* made light work of reaching their seventh finals in a row. The England captain's tireless efforts may sometimes go unnoticed as he does a fine job of wearing defenders down and creating space for his team-mates. Kane is happy to operate in this somewhat selfless role, confident that if a chance comes his way, he is likely to find the back of the net. Don't say that we didn't warn you, goalkeepers!

7

Kane scored a combined seven goals across back-to-back FIFA World Cup qualifiers in November 2021.

Drea_____m

MEMPHIS DEPAY

Country: Netherlands ◆ **Club:** Barcelona
Date of birth: 13 February 1994

🏐 77 caps 👟 39 goals

In recent seasons, Memphis Depay has gone from being a talented forward with bags of potential to a reliable international goalscorer. The Barça frontman struck 12 times in qualifying to match Harry Kane's return and also provided six assists as he demonstrated his importance to the team's attacking play. He is adept at shooting with either foot and has the pace to pull away from defenders in wide areas or through the middle. Opposition defences will have to be particularly alert to his link-up play with Georginio Wijnaldum.

CRISTIANO RONALDO

Country: Portugal ◆ **Club:** Manchester United
Date of birth: 5 February 1985

🏐 186 caps 👟 115 goals

Cristiano Ronaldo tops the men's all-time goal charts in international football, has over 800 career strikes to his name and has netted at 11 international tournaments, including the FIFA Confederations Cup and the UEFA Nations League. He helped to steer Portugal through the play-offs in March and if he manages to get his name on the scoresheet at Qatar 2022, he will become the first male player to have scored at five FIFA World Cups. Ronaldo remains a world-class performer in and around the opposition's box and is set to be one of the main attractions in Qatar.

TIMO WERNER

Country: Germany ◆ **Club:** Chelsea
Date of birth: 6 March 1996

🏐 49 caps 👟 22 goals

Germany were the first country to qualify for Qatar 2022, with Timo Werner, Serge Gnabry and İlkay Gündoğan all weighing in with five goals apiece. Not your traditional out-and-out striker, Werner hits his stride when drifting across the forward line to make the most of his speed and ability to link up with team-mates. The physical side of his game has improved markedly since he made the move to the English Premier League. Most notably, his quick-fire double against North Macedonia in a 4-0 rout away from home helped *Die Mannschaft* secure the win that clinched qualification for the finals.

FIFA World Cup player watch:
MIDFIELDERS

SON HEUNG-MIN

Country: Korea Republic
Club: Tottenham Hotspur
Date of birth: 8 July 1992

98 caps   31 goals

For opposition teams, the famous Korea Republic captain will be one of the toughest players to mark. He is a very attack-focused and versatile player who can operate centrally, out wide or in an advanced forward role to score and create goals. Qatar 2022 will mark Son's third appearance at a FIFA World Cup and, after excelling for English team Tottenham, his name on the team sheet will strike fear into opponents. His close control, powerful shooting and speed with and without the ball mean he will be Korea Republic's main attacking weapon in Group H.

2

Son scored twice at the 2018 FIFA World Cup, with injury-time strikes against Mexico and Germany.

KEVIN DE BRUYNE

Country: Belgium ◆ **Club:** Manchester City
Date of birth: 28 June 1991

88 caps · 23 goals

Kevin De Bruyne makes his midfield mastery look deceptively simple. Preparing to grace the FIFA World Cup for a third time, he is capable of operating as a deep-lying playmaker, a role in which he gets the ball from his defenders before pinging precision passes, but is also comfortable playing off the strikers and drifting into wide areas. He is adept at whipping inviting crosses into the box or picking a clever pass to pierce the opposition defence. De Bruyne is a game-changer and an expert match-winner if ever there was one.

BRUNO FERNANDES

Country: Portugal ◆ **Club:** Manchester United
Date of birth: 8 September 1994

42 caps · 8 goals

In a team blessed with the attacking talents of Cristiano Ronaldo, Diogo Jota and André Silva, Fernandes is the man tasked with creating the play and feeding the forwards. His understanding with Ronaldo has improved immensely since the latter returned to Old Trafford. Fernandes's irresistible delivery and impressive vision mean that Portugal are sure to be a threat in Qatar. He played a total of just 88 minutes at Russia 2018, but four years on, his all-round game and influence have come on in leaps and bounds.

LEON GORETZKA

Country: Germany ◆ **Club:** Bayern Munich
Date of birth: 6 February 1995

41 caps · 14 goals

After Germany became the first team to qualify for Qatar 2022, their versatile midfielder Leon Goretzka claimed that the team "are on the right track to get back to the top of the tree in world football". In fact, Goretzka got Germany's successful campaign off to a flying start by scoring after just three minutes in their opening qualifier in March 2021. Alongside his Bayern Munich team-mate Joshua Kimmich, the 27-year-old has the energy and skills to control a game and has been compared to former Germany greats Lothar Matthäus and Michael Ballack.

FIFA World Cup player watch:
MIDFIELDERS

SERGIO BUSQUETS

Country: Spain ◆ **Club:** Barcelona
Date of birth: 16 July 1988

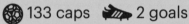

133 caps 🥾 2 goals

While Sergio Busquets' fresh-faced midfield team-mates Pedri and Gavi have been winning all the plaudits for Spain, the veteran's experience and impact should not be overlooked. The defensive midfielder, who has claimed more than 30 domestic and international trophies in his career, including the 2010 FIFA World Cup and UEFA EURO 2012, brings calmness and determined tenacity to Spain's game. Having featured in 13 games across three FIFA World Cups, this wise head with slick feet can be relied on to deliver on the biggest stage once again.

100

Busquets brought up a century of caps in 2017 after making his senior debut in 2009.

JACK GREALISH

Country: England ◆ **Club:** Manchester City
Date of birth: 10 September 1995

🏐 19 caps 👟 1 goal

The exciting Jack Grealish is poised to make his maiden appearance at a FIFA World Cup and will be keen to shine. After securing a headline-grabbing GBP 100m move from Aston Villa to Manchester City in August 2021, the stylish playmaker has continued to impress for both club and country, using his fast feet, strength, speed and smart passing to outfox his opponents. England are truly blessed with some fine attacking midfielders and Grealish has a fight on his hands to hold down a starting spot. Nevertheless, the Birmingham native still represents an enviable option to unleash from off the bench.

PAUL POGBA

Country: France ◆ **Club:** Manchester United
Date of birth: 15 March 1993

🏐 91 caps 👟 11 goals

Paul Pogba scooped the Best Young Player award at the 2014 FIFA World Cup, where he helped France progress to the quarter-finals. *Les Bleus* took the crown in the following edition, with the talismanic Pogba on target in the showpiece. Pogba is capable of producing devastating displays of midfield domination thanks to his height, power, range of passing and shooting accuracy. He missed just two games in the qualifying campaign through injury and coach Didier Deschamps is well aware of the vital role Pogba plays in this France side.

CASEMIRO

Country: Brazil ◆ **Club:** Real Madrid
Date of birth: 23 February 1992

🏐 61 caps 👟 5 goals

For all their creative attacking flair, Brazil still need leaders in the team to provide balance and ensure they are a tough side to break down. The combative Casemiro – who often wears the captain's armband in Thiago Silva's absence – can lay claim to being among the best in the business when it comes to shielding his centre-backs, recovering possession and initiating attacks. What's more, the stalwart is blessed with an impressive engine that allows him to get up and down the pitch. With Casemiro in their line-up, the five-time champions have every chance of making the latter stages.

FIFA World Cup player watch:
DEFENDERS

VIRGIL VAN DIJK

Country: Netherlands ◆ **Club:** Liverpool
Date of birth: 8 July 1991

46 caps   5 goals

The international stage has largely proved frustrating in what has so far been a glittering career for Virgil van Dijk. The Netherlands failed to qualify for UEFA EURO 2016 and were also absent from the most recent edition of the FIFA World Cup. Furthermore, Van Dijk missed out on UEFA EURO 2020 through injury. So, Qatar 2022 represents a massive opportunity for the towering centre-back to make up for the disappointments. As *Oranje* captain, he leads by example and his epic celebrations following the Netherlands' 2-0 win over Norway, which sealed their spot at the finals, showed just how desperate he is to grace this tournament.

2018
The year Van Dijk became national-team captain and notched his first international goal.

HARRY MAGUIRE

Country: England ◆ **Club:** Manchester United
Date of birth: 5 March 1993

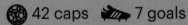 42 caps　　7 goals

Harry Maguire holds fond memories of Russia 2018, where he emerged as a standout performer and was among the goals as the *Three Lions* reached the semi-finals. In the ensuing four years, he has established himself as the key man in England's backline. The Sheffield-born central defender has led the national team to many clean sheets and has also weighed in with headed goals from set pieces. Comfortable playing out from the back, Maguire is not one to be fazed by even the game's most feared international strikers.

RAPHAËL VARANE

Country: France ◆ **Club:** Manchester United
Date of birth: 25 April 1993

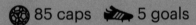 85 caps　　5 goals

The FIFA World Cup, UEFA Nations League, UEFA Champions League... Raphaël Varane has won some of the most coveted prizes in both club and international football. The assured defender revelled in France's trophy success last time round and will be confident of *Les Bleus'* chances of retaining their crown in Qatar. He rarely loses focus on the pitch and has a knack of being in the right place at the right time. These qualities mean that opposing forwards will have to be at the top of their game to beat Varane.

SIMON KJÆR

Country: Denmark ◆ **Club:** AC Milan
Date of birth: 26 March 1989

119 caps　　5 goals

Simon Kjær's name may not spring to some people's minds when one is asked to list the game's top defenders, but a glance at his achievements and performances for Denmark would be enough to convince even the staunchest critic. The Danes booked their ticket to Qatar with two games to spare. What's more, after storming to the UEFA EURO 2020 semi-finals, they will be keen to show the same fortitude on the world's biggest stage. Kjær's composure and leadership were evident at last year's EURO after team-mate Christian Eriksen suffered a cardiac arrest. Displaying the same strength in Qatar will be key to the team's chances of success.

FIFA World Cup player watch:
GOALKEEPERS

THIBAUT COURTOIS

Country: Belgium ◆ **Club:** Real Madrid
Date of birth: 11 May 1992

◎ 94 caps 👟 2011 debut

Having now been a commanding presence in goal for more than a decade for the *Red Devils*, Courtois is ready to play his part in Belgium's quest for FIFA World Cup glory. He starred in the tournament's previous edition, where he won the adidas Golden Glove, and featured five times in qualifying as the Belgians again impressed en route to Qatar. Boasting power, agility, cat-like reflexes and pinpoint kicking accuracy, the Real Madrid keeper really does tick all the boxes.

27
Courtois made 27 saves at Russia 2018, more than any other goalkeeper.

ALISSON

Country: Brazil ◆ **Club:** Liverpool
Date of birth: 2 October 1992

 54 caps 2015 debut

With many of the world's top international teams having adopted a tactic that involves playing the ball out from the back, Alisson has established himself as an exemplar in his position. Not only does his distribution – be it with his feet or his hands – inspire confidence, but he is equally adept at racing off his line to snuff out danger, pulling off a reflex save or plucking a cross from out of the air. Alisson faces stiff competition from Manchester City's Ederson for Brazil's no. 1 jersey, but this is likely to drive him on to raise his game. Come what may, Brazil can rest assured that their team will be in safe hands at Qatar 2022.

MANUEL NEUER

Country: Germany ◆ **Club:** Bayern Munich
Date of birth: 27 March 1986

 109 caps 2009 debut

Even at 36, Manuel Neuer is still widely regarded as a world-class goalkeeper and is poised to play a pivotal role in Germany's bid to capture their fifth FIFA World Cup crown. Neuer's calming presence allows his defenders to go and apply a high press, while confident that their goalie will deal with any balls in behind. Though Barcelona's Marc-André ter Stegen is pushing the Bayern glovesman hard for a place in the starting line-up, Neuer is not ready to call time on his international career just yet.

UNAI SIMÓN

Country: Spain ◆ **Club:** Athletic Bilbao
Date of birth: 11 June 1997

 21 caps 2020 debut

Only two years into his international career with *La Roja*, Unai Simón has already featured at UEFA EURO 2020, where he saved penalties in shoot-outs against Switzerland and Italy, and played his part as Spain reached the final at both the Men's Olympic Football Tournament Tokyo 2020 and the UEFA Nations League. In the build-up to his maiden FIFA World Cup, the Basque custodian will need to continue to deliver the same levels of consistency so as to fend off competition from David de Gea and Kepa Arrizabalaga, but he is in the box seat to help his country to the latter stages of another major tournament.

FIFA World Cup quiz part 1

Time to put your World Cup knowledge to the ultimate test. There are 200 points up for grabs and the answers are on page 61. Good luck, folks!

1. PENALTY SPOT

France striker Antoine Griezmann strikes a penalty at Russia 2018, but which of these is the real ball?

Ball A ◇   Ball D ◇

Ball B ✓   Ball E ◇

Ball C ◇

10 points for the correct answer

2. CAPTAIN CLOSE-UP

The camera has zoomed in on four captains who successfully led their countries to Qatar 2022. Can you name the captains? Read each clue and write your answer below.

A
My initials are HK.

B
I played in the 2018 FIFA World Cup final.

C
I own a FIFA World Cup winners' medal.

D
I have also captained a Premier League club side.

ran

mabvoch lores

van

10 points for each correct answer

58

3. HOST PARTY

Can you name the last time the following countries hosted the FIFA World Cup? Write the year below each country.

Germany   **Italy**   **Brazil**

....

10 points for each correct answer

4. SCORED OR SAVED?

The photos below show Poland's Robert Lewandowski and Belgium's Eden Hazard in action at Russia 2018. Did they score or were their shots saved?

LEWANDOWSKI:

Scored ☑

Saved ☑

HAZARD:

Scored ☑

Saved ☑

10 points for each correct answer

FIFA World Cup quiz part 2

5. SPOT THE DIFFERENCE

Below is an image of Argentina booking their place at Qatar 2022. Five changes have been made to the second picture. Circle them all.

5 points for each difference found

6. PLAYER PICK

Germany and the Netherlands are famous FIFA World Cup rivals. Can you pick out the five Dutch players from the list below, which features star names from both teams?

KLAASSEN

HAVERTZ

DE LIGT

REUS

BLIND

BERGWIJN

DUMFRIES

MÜLLER

5 points for each correct answer

7. TEAM TALK

The three facts below refer to one of the teams taking part in Qatar 2022. Read the clues and work out who the mystery team are.

They reached the round of 16 at Russia 2018.

They topped their qualifying group ahead of Sweden.

Álvaro Morata is one of their stars.

....

10 points for the correct answer

8. SCORER SEARCH

Hidden in the grid are the names of ten players who have scored at a FIFA World Cup. Look for them all!

O	A	G	U	E	R	O	P	F	Z
I	N	A	R	D	P	L	E	E	U
I	R	I	Q	A	H	S	R	Z	C
U	I	R	M	V	S	A	I	A	M
T	N	A	S	R	U	D	S	Q	A
G	Y	M	A	S	I	M	I	A	G
I	V	I	L	M	P	F	C	B	U
L	K	D	A	J	H	A	G	G	I
E	G	U	H	B	R	F	L	O	R
C	I	V	O	R	T	I	M	P	E

SALAH   **SUÁREZ**   **SHAQIRI**

MITROVIĆ   **AGÜERO**   **DI MARÍA**

FIRMINO   **PERIŠIĆ**   **MAGUIRE**

POGBA

4 points for each player found

My final score

..../200

Your match schedule and results chart

Record the results of all 64 group-stage and knockout games from the FIFA World Cup Qatar 2022. The tournament kicks off on 21 November.

GROUP A

21 Nov, 16:00	Qatar	0	2	Ecuador	Al Bayt
21 Nov, 10:00	Senegal	0	2	Netherlands	Al Thumama
25 Nov, 13:00	Qatar	1	3	Senegal	Al Thumama
25 Nov, 16:00	Netherlands	1	1	Ecuador	Khalifa International
29 Nov, 15:00	Ecuador	1	2	Senegal	Khalifa International
29 Nov, 15:00	Netherlands	2	0	Qatar	Al Bayt

Team	P	W	D	L	GD	Pts

GROUP B

21 Nov, 13:00	England	6	2	IR Iran	Khalifa Int.
21 Nov, 19:00	USA	1	1	Wales	Ahmad Bin Ali
25 Nov, 10:00	Wales			IR Iran	Ahmad Bin Ali
25 Nov, 19:00	England	0	0	USA	Al Bayt
29 Nov, 19:00	Wales	0	3	England	Ahmad Bin Ali
29 Nov, 19:00	IR Iran	0	0	USA	Al Thumama

Team	P	W	D	L	GD	Pts

GROUP C

22 Nov, 16:00	Mexico	0	0	Poland	Stadium 974
22 Nov, 10:00	Argentina	1	2	Saudi Arabia	Lusail
26 Nov, 13:00	Poland	2	0	Saudi Arabia	Education City
26 Nov, 19:00	Argentina	2	0	Mexico	Lusail
30 Nov, 19:00	Poland	0	2	Argentina	Stadium 974
30 Nov, 19:00	Saudi Arabia			Mexico	Lusail

Team	P	W	D	L	GD	Pts

GROUP D

22 Nov, 19:00	France	4	1	Australia	Al Janoub
22 Nov, 13:00	Denmark			Tunisia	Education City
26 Nov, 10:00	Tunisia	0	0	Denmark	Al Janoub
26 Nov, 16:00	France	2	1	Denmark	Stadium 974
30 Nov, 15:00	Australia	1	0	Denmark	Al Janoub
30 Nov, 15:00	Tunisia	2	1	France	Education City

Team	P	W	D	L	GD	Pts

GROUP E

23 Nov, 16:00	Spain	7	0	Costa Rica	Al Thumama
23 Nov, 13:00	Germany	1	2	Japan	Khalifa International
27 Nov, 10:00	Japan	0	1	Costa Rica	Ahmad Bin Ali
27 Nov, 19:00	Spain	1	1	Germany	Al Bayt
1 Dec, 19:00	Japan	2	1	Spain	Khalifa International
1 Dec, 19:00	Costa Rica	2	4	Germany	Al Bayt

Team	P	W	D	L	GD	Pts

GROUP F

23 Nov, 19:00	Belgium	2	0	Canada	Ahmad Bin Ali
23 Nov, 10:00	Morocco	2	0	Croatia	Al Bayt
27 Nov, 13:00	Belgium	0	2	Morocco	Al Thumama
27 Nov, 16:00	Croatia	2	2	Canada	Khalifa International
1 Dec, 15:00	Croatia	2	1	Belgium	Ahmad Bin Ali
1 Dec, 15:00	Canada	2	1	Morocco	Al Thumama

Team	P	W	D	L	GD	Pts

All kick-off times are in GMT.